BURNING STONE

OTHER BOOKS BY ZOË LANDALE

Harvest of Salmon (Hancock House)

Shop Talk (Pulp Press, edited)

Colour of Winter Air (Sono Nis)

BURNING STONE

Poems

by

Zoë Landale

RONSDALE/CACANADADADA

1995

RONSDALE PRESS
3350 West 21st Avenue
Vancouver, BC, Canada
V6S 1G7

Typeset by The Typeworks in ITC New Baskerville, 11 pt on 13½
Printing: Hignell Printing, Winnipeg, Manitoba
Author photo: Jane Weitzel
Cover Design: Cecilia Jang
Cover Art: Don Jarvis "Fire Theme"
Cover Photo: Courtesy of Bau-Xi Gallery, Vancouver, BC

The publisher wishes to thank the Canada Council and the British Columbia Cultural Services Branch for their financial assistance.

CANADIAN CATALOGUING IN PUBLICATION DATA

Landale, Zoë, 1952-
   Burning Stone

   Poems.
   ISBN 0–921870–31–0

   I. Title.
PS8573.A5315B87   1995   C811'.54   C94–910866–9
PR9199.3.L36B87   1995

Dedicated to Garney Coburn,
who convinced me I could say
"No, this is not my story,"
and to the ghosts.

ACKNOWLEDGEMENTS

Some of these poems have been published in or accepted by
the following magazines and anthologies: *The Malahat Review,
Pottersfield Portfolio, Prairie Fire, CV2, The Capilano Review, Cana-
dian Literature, TickleAce, Fiddlehead, Fireweed, The Prairie Journal,
the literary hot girls review* (U.S.), *Vintage '93* (The League of Ca-
nadian Poets), *The Windhorse Reader: Choice Poems of '93* (Samu-
rai Books).

Translation from the Latin courtesy of Mark Warrior.

Special thanks to George McWhirter.

Contents

MY BEAUTIFUL GHOSTS

POSE

Here we are arranged
into set-pieces on the sofa.
Manners by mother,
& temper by Dad.
Fear all our own.

I am fourteen, the eldest.
I sit with one knee
crossed, hands held in the lap
in closed, palm-on-palm gesture that says
Oh really?
We three girls have put on
hauteur for the camera,
formally assumed mouths
though the youngest's socks
have collapsed at her ankles like panting dogs
& her skirt bunches at the waist.

Our brother gazes at something invisible
on the shag rug.
His downed white lids
give him the look of someone asleep
or dreaming of stillness,
a lizard
lit green glass on a sunny wall.
Somewhere far
from here.
Far from the shouting that will resume
within moments after the *snick*
of the shutter.

The middle girl has round
cheeks & eyes that narrow warily.
She whirls
from one locus of strong emotion
to the next, a compass needle
pulled by forces
for which she has no name.
She will die
when she is twenty without
a word.
In the photograph, she looks guilty
already.

"THERE'S SOMETHING YOU
SHOULD KNOW..."

When my mother says this
in a certain tone
I dilate with dread
from cold toes up.
Something means family.
She's about to pluck a dead
bird-secret,
clammy in pinfeathers beside my breakfast
of toast & honey.

(The horrible singey-smell
as we burn the feathers off.)

There's something
she feels I should know
to set the record straight.
I want to fly.
She wants response,
between us to stitch
the ripped bird.

Family a carcass, a mountain,
I don't want to struggle up,
family a wound I can't heal.
Family coagulated.
Family too early in the morning.
My mother's voice,
approaching feathers:
the whole day dangles.

HOSTING STORIES

Mostly the stories are not visible, wear us like shirts of
Indian cotton, printed with interlocking paisleys: reds,
purples, golds   We think their swaggering is our
own   Often they fit us so well—or we them—there is no
gap between what they tell us, what we believe   The tiny
mirrors on cloth show nothing but colour, the swish of
movement

but now & then we catch ghosts reflected in them, telling
stories

Stories we realize are not our own   Stories handed
down   Stories in the air, ones grandparents grew up
hearing, details mainly lost after a hundred years, but the
basic elements remain: a woman's shining waist-length hair,
the scent of roses, of invitation & finally, violent
death   Stories whose plot we fall into like brine,
unsurprised at the sting, the chill & harsh black rising in
our throats   Stories as dangerous strangers whom we
realize that too late we should never have invited
home   Stories like hands about our necks

Hosting the stories   Hosting the ghosts, making them
welcome, they are family aren't they?   Hosting our kin
who speak the same radiant metaphors—we laugh at the
same jokes   Hosting gardens with kale and potatoes in
abundant rows   Hosting as well the familiar shadows on
the wall, the scary animals

I get people to tell me their story, the writer on the bus
said   She was white & sweet as the inside of a crisp
apple, dressed in hand-woven pinks *Everyone has their story, it
can be a sentence, "I was the second-eldest & always left
out"*   *The mark of our real stories is they recur*

& it is the ghosts of course, telling us they believe

we are monsters or doomed, because it runs in the
family   Stories fuel us like engines made of blood, or
roses, red & ticking over petal by petal, disintegration
predictable as piston strokes   Hosting the long lies of
others' lives, the slow toppling into concealed
stories   Hosting the seeded greenery, the roots of *I am
alone & afraid*
Stories that run quick as blight through furrows of
leaves   Stories that grapple with us, take over   Stories
that push us into the boarded-up well   Our hands, pale
& luminous, show above the salt water, waving for help
that is late, late in coming: we suffocate, the kale is too
tough & we cannot breathe the unwelcoming dark

We think it is our own difficult lives that haunt us, see
ourselves as separate from families, strike out determined to
do things right, dismiss the winking of silvered metal as
false coinage, purple reflections; straighten our shoulders,
wish for ironed cloth smooth on the skin   Mostly we are
used to the trickery of our lives

Only sometimes we hear the stories afresh, look to see what
narrative dangles us from its hook
& ask can we bend the metal, shrug off our shirts & walk
away?

EDITHA FORD BEAUFORT

I will do anything but write where the past ends again on
my Great-grandmother's ragged rope. Jocelyn, age five and
a half, reaches out to hold Editha's photograph, a fine-
boned woman, defiant somehow with a swirled topknot,
springy hair, a jewelled pin on the collar of her pouffed &
exquisite white dress. *I will not,* she seems to be vibrating. I
wonder what she is so resentful about. "She doesn't look
very happy, Mummy," says Jocelyn.

Outside my window, a toddler pulls a woman across
Fisherman's Hall parking lot. Gravel & clanging July sun.
Blue flowers on her dress shout electrically across my retina
long after they disappear. Have I written enough now, I
wonder, can I pick roses for pot-pourri? Editha's eyes are
too much like my sister's, that snap of intelligence, blaze of
all-there & not liking it.

To call her *Great-grandmother* pushes her away, makes her
innocuously dead. But this unsmiling face of less than thirty
is profoundly here, un-safe, rams fear down my gullet deep
as a shark hook, says, *Why not wake up one morning—make it
today—& kill yourself? Why not leave kids crying, a husband to
choke on your name for years? The world is so dangerous, so
monstrous, you must leave everything right now & run, run for death
as though it were silver water & life a fire forty feet tall crackling at
your heels, leap for that silver blessed cold.*

& no one living can tell me why you would jump, Editha.

Your eyes say my sister is in danger, anyone is who looks
too long into bleak fire. I say you're wrong. Despair is
deliberately drawing opacity over your heart. You come to
a point where you refuse to understand, stand sullen as a
tree refusing to grow, knowing something is required of
you. Did you refuse to give up the imperiousness that
makes your mouth so thin? My sister has stared into the
roar & hiss you knew but her mouth relents, she's coming
back from the edge. Ghosts? She rides a shaggy Appaloosa
through them, canters soaking wet along rainforest trails,
returns to drink coffee with the rude & living.

"Little mummy," your youngest daughter, Minnie, my
grandmother, called you in her diary. She kept track of
your birthday: "Bless you little mummy, wherever you
are." Minnie was seven when you died. Wherever you
have gone, did you jerk when she wrote Happy Birthday
year after year? Did you see Minnie as a hummingbird
brushing the red funnel of a fuchsia, yourself a world of
furled colour, drooping?

My father tells me you hung yourself. Gruesome. I chide
myself for wanting to know, but it's of a piece, the why, the
how, your handsome husband & the three girls couldn't
keep you alight or soften that pale flame of self which stares
up daring me, what? After a hundred years, what gives you
power—that rope smack smacking the palm of your
invisible hand?

MY BEAUTIFUL GHOSTS

They are all beautiful, these ancestors.
I shuffle faces through my hands
the dissatisfied, the ardent.
I have waited for these ghosts in my office
to enlighten me
about what makes breathing important.
They only
pose
more questions.
It upsets me, having them here
in ancient brown suede frames, vitality
thrusting out
into yielding air.
Circa 1850, the photograph
of my sixteen-year old Great-great grandmother states.
Burned onto paper, these people are recognizable forces
I might have met at the writers' potluck last week.
Only their clothes give them away,
strange stiff dresses the women wear.
My Great-grandmother's eyeglasses
have no arms, cling
dauntingly tight
to her nose.
My young grandfather's portrait
has a long dashingly-written inscription,

Magistro suo, qui summa benevolentia ac humanitate puero improbo
usus est. Hanc imaginem, toga virili iam assumpta, donat haud
     ingratos.
Ante diem septum kalendas Octobres, anno post Christum natum
     MCMXll.
"To his master, who has treated an unworthy child with
the greatest benevolence and humanity, he gives this
picture, having already put on his adult toga, not
ungratefully.
The seventh day before the end of October, 1912."

On the floor one large box of photographs
spills, another of papers;
they scald
deceivingly as steam.
By the time I realize how their lives will hurt
it is too late to draw back my hands.
My grandmother Minnie's diaries from 1917 to 1979 pulse
& the letters, many written
by my beautiful ghosts,
fine-featured small men & women who flare
from shelves & floor, where I have propped their faces,
a gallery of blazing family.
Worn family who rock the room with insinuations
about illegitimacy, who drank too much,
who died because they wanted to.
Who jumped from a second-storey window
onto an iron picket fence?

I dread climbing the stairs
to work.
I am too solid
all of me listens.

For every question I ask, the ghosts fling
three back: sparks delicate & incendiary as they claim
their lives were.
When my father said they weighed
on him, he meant their faces
came too close.
Who they were
burns who we are, daily.
They consume us.

Later, at Christmas, my brother will say across the table,
Oh, the Simmins & Beauforts are an interesting family,
all right.
That's the mythology, how interesting we are, how vital.
Other people pale beside us.
Alcoholism, incest, child abuse . . .
Jesus Christ! What a price
the innocent pay for our genius.
I argue about incest,
concede the rest. *Who do we remember?*
my brother asks, unforgiving
of our father where the indulgence
of Grand Passion at any cost
meant our cost, our childhood.
The public servants? No. The false glory of bad guys.
Richard Dangerfield Simmins, the gambler,
whose brother had to sell his medical practice
in Edinburgh & emigrate to Australia
to cover his debts.

I think of what our father said:
You come from a long line of horse thieves & priests.
Fed-up with melodrama, my brother
bends his formidable will toward
being rock-solid & decent
as he thinks our mother's people were.
I don't tell him she says
they were as nutty as the stuffing
he just ate at dinner.

What my beautiful ghosts ask
is not for me to gutter
& char in their blaze,
necessarily,
but to come closer, endure
the conflagration
until it becomes light.

I'm not sure I can stand
all these sharp wills
igniting
in me.
Slow explosion of recognitions,
living relatives grinning in long-dead faces.
I'd like to believe we make our own history.

> *History*, the ghosts echo.
> *Would we have made so many mistakes*
> *if we had recognized ourselves as bound*
> *to the incendiary belief*
> *of no past,*
> *no myths but our own*
> *self-created ones?*
>
> *We're your family, trust us*
> *to tell our story of fire.*

GRANDFATHERS ARE ANATHEMA

Grandfathers are for raging at
safely, now they are eyesockets & pelvic girdles.
Stories of their casual violence emerge
unmistakeable as bones poking
out from gravel by a creek.
One beat my husband until he forgot
everything but the terror
of the man.
He was mean to Peggy,
chased her around the house with a flyswatter.
He kept on hitting her.
Peggy, five years older, looks at me with seal-eyes
(I want to hug away the brown fused hurt), says:
No, it was Garney he was after, he was only three,
he doesn't remember.
Momentarily, I see this stumpy dentist
with the bald head
as Satan.
Sunday afternoon violence, the house heaving with sobs
when he finished
the children, motherless & shaking in their rooms,
not bothering him,
finally,
because it was easier for him
to reach out in anger than in love.
For this grandfather, smoking cigarettes on the porch,
I wish the children's anguish would
descend on him with the same blank horror
of being wrong,
small & unable to escape the *thunk*
of connection as someone else's arm rises,
rises again.

My grandfather (curse his civilized reading
of Latin classics on cross-Canada train trips)
molested my uncle, his favourite son
first-born
first to die, a suicide.
These men set me spinning
with rage:
their greeds stick in my throat, choking.
They thought no one would know
of their quick indulgences, soon
over,
that they were the fulcrum
around which the malleable world swung.
The world contracted
to their own urgent
wants.
These grandfathers thought right was not solid enough
to lean on.
The hardness they inflicted
would never be uncovered,
that their violations
were as inconsequential as throwing
stones.
They could toss whatever they wanted
until their arms grew tired.

Water covers a multitude of sins.

Water recedes.
Water clears.
Children tell, some fifty years later,
about the awful bones by the creek,
the claws.
Grandfathers, I spit
on your remains.

You are short men
smaller in stature than even you thought.
Believe me, from this angle
my eyes see with no trace ·
of fluttering iridescent sentiment,
flags flying of *He meant well* . . .
You have to remember . . .
There are no
excuses.
Your names have become anathema:
I rip your photographs
your yellowed smiles
from my heart.

GRANDMOTHERS ARE FOR HITTING

Grandmothers are for hitting
until I am silly
with judgments, though their days no doubt
seemed much like any other
to those swimming through them.
On the radio, news of riots, assassinations,
trouble:
the Suez crisis, the Cuban missile crisis reaching out
to darken cloud-slippery mornings.
If war breaks out . . . Minnie writes in her journal.
My father, her son, says to her,
You'll come back here, where there's a basement.
If worst comes to worst, I can shoot the family.
My poor grandmother
tossed sleepless on her bed, a stranded dolphin
until the world eased back
to deep sea, illusion of streaming ahead again.
My past has many mouths
all of them
closed
against motion of water
or full of ancient hurts.
Years of mornings where the sun
never does come out.
This grandmother didn't protect her children.
That one spent forty years clipping
ends off moments.
I can't figure out
what she did with them,

nor if I have any right to
climb inside
reconstructed skins of family history,
examine them
for dry flakes of fiction,
happy-endings.

PHOTOMONTAGE

One black & white snapshot in particular
snags me.
It is of my family having tea on the lawn
sixty years earlier.
August afternoon. My grandmother wears
a short-sleeved dress, looks querulous;
I think of the *cor-roo, cor-roo*
of a mourning dove, flitting long-tailed,
edgy, from tree to tree.
Stupidly, beaming, I bend my head
to enter the tiny world of arrested cheer
as if I believe details
will save me.

The word *family* has misled me.
I had hoped for kisses
all round
affection heady as brandy
in late westerly sun,
a cup of tea
& cucumber-breath hugs

but there is no safety in these people.

The past
slaps
so hard
I see white lightning
snake
all along one cheek.

I came to this stilled afternoon
hoping to carry clues away,
a neat package wrapped in cardboard:
why do I fear
so much?
It is a long way
to reach for the marrow
& find it still warm
with the resistant texture of caramel.
These people wear faces
borrowed
from a history I thought my own;
my middle sister, dead at twenty,
my former husband who wanted hours immense as cumulus
so I could work longer.
On this day of sticky heat
my grandmother
is three years older
than I am now.
She looks like my sister, sly
& fat-cheeked.
My grandfather is so like my husband
I wince, wonder who it was
exactly
I fell for.

My father is a child of seven.
I watch him—
beautiful, even-featured, wary,
still alive.
Years from now, my uncle will leave
his wife & children survivors
in name only
after he locks himself in his car
with the engine running, exhaust blocked.
I am afraid of hurting you his note will say.

Implosive irony; my cousins
will swim in stunted circles.
For them, always the threat
of ugly morning looms,
a car big as the world.

I stare at the raised cheer of teacups,
hard shade.
Even on this hot day, my grandfather
wears a jacket & tie.
He read Horace in Latin,
ended his letters to my grandmother
Beloved, I kiss thy feet.
He beat his children so they dimpled
soft as red cedar,
never meant for hammering.

One night when my father is ten
& it is snowing, he will find my grandfather
drunk in a snowdrift
& will think *No one will ever know*
if I leave him here.
I could just keep walking
How much easier it would be
for all of us . . .
Ashamed he could think this
& that it is true, my father
whose eyes are still as blue, as visionary
as the child he was,
will pluck his father out of the drift,
chivy him home to warmth.
Many times my father will relive
that weighted instant,
each snowy step
before
he put out a hand.

This is ahead of them, I know, but
only by a few years
& meantime the sun is August.
My family watches me with such purity,
such intensity
I want to cry
for what they will endure.
The rough grass needs clipping.
They smile in the Quebec heat.
A wing of my grandmother's greying hair
flutters.
I would give them something, anything
to help with what is coming
but all I can offer
is my presence now, years later,
when I will bear anxious witness
to their struggles.

My father watches me
from another photograph, age ten,
as a grave child with falling-down socks.
When he was sixty-five, he said to me
People do the best they can.
This I will hold,
weighty
& smooth as yellow whale bone.

FAMILY

THE OLD VITRIOL

for my father

Your contempt for all my mother's family, *Atkinson, Glass,*
pressing them flat & ridiculous as johnny-jump-ups in a
family Bible, faded yellows & purples route-maps of long-
vanished summers leading nowhere, their prominence &
brighter strokes of flower veins   When the pages were
turned, the dry blooms would flake out of the book,
transparencies distressingly visible

Josie was a Good Christian   Cecil a Nice Man
Lorraine, well, she was A Beauty when she was younger
      Air would thicken, waiting for more, for precise
deficiencies to be high-lighted & I would join the game of
finding fault with relatives, eagerly correct shapes that were
not like ours   Cruelty never entered our minds, we were
being observant

BUT *Josie had a nervous breakdown during the First World War,
she says she couldn't nurse again because of her hands but it's all up
here, the shaking, you know*
BUT *Cece is probably the dullest man I've ever met, God, & that
awful boat he built*   Hey, I say, ten years old, indignant
that magic is being broken, wonder of heading off across
Lake Ontario in a rush of opalescent blue July *I think the
boat is pretty neat   Sure & first he had to take off the basement
door to get the thing out & that didn't work, so he had to take down
a whole wall, can you imagine what that must have cost? He could
have bought a DECENT boat for the money*
BUT *Lorraine has never got along with your mother, do you know
what she did the last time she came out?* & you would tell a
funny, indignant story about what a bad sister Lorraine
was   It changed over the years; now you say she took
fourteen-year-old boys to bed

Laughing is fun   Clever people are fun   Clever people
laugh

You write & say how much you enjoyed my last letter
about the literary celebrity I met & her husband, my prose
so nicely-done the cuts barely hurt her & it's me who feels
pain, I didn't mean to skewer her, it must have happened
on automatic pilot   & I wonder what kind of hybrid I
would resemble if laughing people looked for my flaws,
grafted them cleverly together & had fun

Stodgy, respectable, dull, worthy, & *middle-class*, mother's
people always remained Other to you—   Here's a
thought for the middle of the night, are all of us kids half-
Other?   Or have we been brought up with enough
tragedy to be acceptably glamorous?   To earn our last
name?   I changed mine

You are known as a sweet man (a description you dislike),
one with great patience toward the afflicted & artists, but
you worry about me becoming too kind   My last letter
reassures you, I am able to dissect up-jumping-johnnies
still, with the finest of acid strokes   *The old vitriol is still
there, my dear,* you write   *Another of your strengths*

AUNT ANNE, ARTIST

1

When I was eight, you broke seeing into pieces for me, bits
of bright delight differentiated from the world-ball of
background, a monarch butterfly tiger on pink
milkweed   The shape of one leaf in a green haze of
identical bushes to be exclaimed over, praised, prised out
for our eyes   *Look at this,* you kept saying *Look*

At sixteen I was hollow-hearted as a blown-glass calla lily,
the kind I saw once in an expensive craft store, coveted, but
didn't know how to get home   I walked stiff-legged out
to the plane, spent the summer with you, learned how to
model with wax, open a can of Campbell's soup for lunch
for my two young cousins, you would be off exulting in the
long grass of your art   *No thanks,* you'd say when I
offered "bean with bacon" soup, *I just want to finish this . . .*

Before supper, you'd offer me a huge glass of sherry with
ice and a squeeze of lime, I'd accept and feel blissfully
warm & grown-up around the edges   My uncle Red no
longer a presence in the boathouse; the summer I was eight
and came for a visit, he'd stay all day in its shadowed
interior & sip beer   *My medicine,* he said, melancholy & I
was sorry I couldn't get him to come out, he was so much
fun at Christmas with his guitar & the boisterous warmth
he'd bring into our house like a great southerly wind

You took me to visit his grave, an unmarked granite stone
in the Rosseau cemetery   An Anne of Green Gables
heroine, I had collected sweet williams to take with us,
realized with shame in the midst of stem-snapping that I
was festooning drama about myself, garnet-red & scented of
cloves   We drove through the woods, slash & whip of
gold through green, a ringing-sun summer morning & all I
could think was how Red would have liked this day if he'd
stayed around to see it   Perhaps it would surprise him
too, if he knew the day had gone on without him

2

You separated beliefs & emotions neatly as a trout's
backbone peels away from cooked flesh   What a
wonderful trick, I thought, words as forks, sliding in to
push away the event   We followed the ways of salt, the
tears I would not cry   You gave me pastels & newsprint
which I filled with black & red   *Good,* you said, *you're
expressing anger*

The child I lost to an abortionist grieved like lemon in a
years'-long cut

Recovering, I lay on rounded rocks & baked, borrowed a
hundred Agatha Christie's from the cottage next door where
no one lived & you had the key, made family mythology in
neon when the boyfriend I thought was two thousand miles
away in Vancouver stood dirty & hot over my lawnchair,
ah True Love at sixteen

3

Last year when you were seventy & I was at a paid-for
conference in Toronto, I took you out for breakfast at the
Four Seasons   Madcap as chickadees, almost penniless,
we laughed & laughed, the coffee shop a warmth we basked
in briefly & with delight   You brought me a painted
calabash from Africa, news of my cousin Tim in the
Caribbean & the hurricane   My heart a Chinese gong,
round brass at how indomitable you were, still planning
another show, teaching, you continued in remission, you
said

Was I sure I could afford to treat you?   I felt such
buoyancy, all these balloons we were launching, we drank
more tea & the two of us fizzed light as we talked family,
talked healing

4

Last week I got up one morning & knew it was time to
send you an azalea   *No colour in particular,* I said when
the florist asked, *get them to send the best-budded they have*

The mid-winter azalea is in celebration of looking   May
it comfort with words of colour, pink or white rejoicing

WHY MY UNCLE RED KILLED HIMSELF

Six years after, his wife Anne said, *He died because of the drug treatments he was receiving, LSD in higher & higher doses; it was legal then, a psychiatrist treated him for war trauma, can you imagine?* Gold hoop earrings, short brown hair, she throws her hands out.

Anne still believes in the gospel of therapy; we talk r.d. laing, ventilation, how the colour red expresses anger.

I do not handle drugs well. I see air go crystalline & hard for Red, the dense flowery patterns which steal into eyes, flat surfaces. What is flat? Ground rises to become vertical when he walks, he's not falling, no, it's coming up to meet him.   & the terrors, they solidify too, I see them crawl sinuous from corners, three-dimensional black snakes flaying the wrapping from reality.

His brother, my father, says: *The poor son-of-a-bitch had his tank blown up from beneath him, not once but twice. It was very unusual for any of the tank crew to survive, you know. It came back to him. & of course his alcoholism didn't help.* Dad drags hard on his cigarette, squints.

His mother, Minnie, wrote: *RIP. No words. No words.* Her diary long stretches of white paper, great invisible wings. Grief comes beating out from the empty pages where day after day she couldn't write.

That night I sat in the hallway with the red carpet where
the phone was & cried. Dad was on the phone, sitting in
the hall chair saying *No, No,* and all that long evening, the
world cracked and dark came in. I sat with my back
against the wall and thought, *Remember the bookcases filled
with paperbacks, the blind whiteness of my father's face, woolly red
of the hall runner, dog hairs on it, edges of hardwood which needed
polishing.*

Red was in their car, dead of carbon monoxide poisoning.
Anguish repeated with the soft mattedness of the rug, the
folding of hands over my chest as if sorrow were a bird with
a tearing beak I kept away. I sat in the hallway long after
Dad went into the bedroom & shut the door. There seemed
no reason to move.

An old Army comrade-in-arms of Red's, Joe Levitt, received
the Military Medal for valour. *A war hero,* Dad says. In the
photograph in "Canadian Jews in World War ll" Levitt
looks like Red. Levitt's resolute face under a dark beret
tweaks my heart, a young man you'd want to trust with
anything, except perhaps a daughter.

Twenty-eight years later, Joe asks Dad over lunch: *So why
did Red kill himself?*

Dad: *Neurosis, alcoholism, the LSD treatments which totally
destroyed any reality he could hold onto.*

Joe: *I think he killed himself because he discovered he was gay. It
was a dreadful, criminal thing in those days; he couldn't face it.*

Dad writes me. I am the Guardian of Secrets. He thinks
Levitt could be right. There are letters, now destroyed,
friendship with someone when Red was 15, and of course
Granddad Nick's nightly incursions. Perhaps singular,
though this is unlikely. There was only one Red's mother
found out about. Loudly.

I read the letter three times. Dad talks about boxes of war-time letters in the basement. There's not much more left to come out, he says. Only details.

Why else, Levitt asks, *would Red have had a man staying with him that last weekend of his life? Anne wasn't there.* Levitt shakes his head, a big man still, despite his heart surgery. He abounds with good humour.

We have pictures of Anne's last visit: she is silver-haired, three inches shorter than she used to be, and distinguished in hand-woven lavenders. She took me out to a gourmet macrobiotic restaurant for dinner. I didn't know there was such a thing.

Anne said she was behind the psychiatric treatments Red received, though of course she had no idea they would go so fearfully wrong. Red wanted to leave her, and their two young children. *BUT you have to see a psychiatrist first & then let's see what you think,* she said.

Anne said Red wanted to leave her for another woman.

Do not trust me to have the last word on their worlds.

Nothing any of you give me is secret. I may forget, I may distort unless I write it down quickly. My imagination falls off edges. I will not carry black weights. I give the burden of them, gratefully, to the lovely open hands of paper.

KAREN IN THE KITCHEN AGAIN

This is a poem for my sister who died
leaving me witness
before the temple
of her destruction.

This is the sister I see eating butter in the kitchen,
black eye-makeup seeping down her cheeks
while I lock my bedroom door
pound hands over an emptied heart.

This is butter which stays dripping
for the seventeen years since her overdose,
until the sight of it, melting again on toast
makes me want to break the frame

of frozen vision. I gave love
which my sister would have sold instantly
if it were worth anything; she stole
clothes, records, whatever presents I was given.

It would be more comfortable to love
than to remember Karen eating butter, taking tenderness,
catching me with a wet dishcloth smack
in my face.

This is the grief, then, how familiar it feels
to think of her without love, butter dripping
from her mouth. I want the frame to soften.
Sister, sister, I implore you:

Give me warm eyes to remember you whole.

RUMINATIONS ON AN ADULT SIB CONTRACT

1.) The NFB movie when you were twelve. I only saw it
years later on a sheet screen in Mum's living room, you
wearing a purple shirt and galloping down Spanish Banks
on your horse. You had long long hair and the saddest face.
I felt my heart turn.
it hasn't worked. Words. Worries. I was wrong, I can see that

to begin. From what I can gather, you've been angry with
me for   The aggrieved party is allowed to tell the
aggriever this whole mess is their fault, one hundred
percent. If the aggriever says anything in reply, it's obvious
she is not sufficiently repentant. Apologies by the aggriever
are to be met with incredulity.

2.) *My love, I wish I could get you to listen. I'm sorry. I didn't*
The aggriever is allowed to defend her/ himself. The
aggrieved
I'm not sure I can give. You want unconditional approval from
has to be quiet and listen to all the good reasons there were
for the incident. No one has to believe this self-justification,
but it's traditional to leave space for it.

I didn't like you going off to school with no breakfast, so
I'd cook bacon and eggs, enough for two; the smell was
supposed to help you get up. And I'd bring you a mug of
tea, strong, with milk and sugar in it. Once I found you,
eyes closed, drumming your feet on the floor—from bed—so
I'd think you were up.
What's so difficult now, is knowing how to stop the recriminations

3.) *left Mortfield Road and that security forever, fed you dinner after*
The sibs can always throw up their hands in horror and
abandon contact. It's expected that after forty years they
will initiate a tearful reconciliation.

You like to come in laughing, with presents, children's pink
pants and a flowered pink and blue shirt, *au courant,* and
you will not stay, it is always spur of the moment and the
moment goes on empty of us.

4.) *years. I've judged you, fussed over you, done all kinds of older*
Stiff and formal contact can be maintained within the
family. Each person shall be careful to talk about trivialities
and mention decisions only after the fact. The aggrieved
will always be "pretty busy right now," too busy to drop
over or come for supper.

When I came to the city, you'd always cook me an
enormous T-bone. I like steak. What amused me was that
you always seemed surprised at the pink, dripping beef we
lifted to our mouths, "I'm not generally keen on it," you'd
say.
sister things, hedged you in with fears to keep you safe and

5.) The aggrieved and the aggriever can sit down for a talk,
but there will be certain proscribed subjects. No comment
except the most glowingly favourable can be made on the
other's choice of mate/companion.
*though, it seems important to make a stand. Why must we pretend
so?* Likewise, nothing shall be said about the mate/
companion's behaviour unless it is to the credit of that
person.
man whom I seem to make most uncomfortable. I'm sorry. Sometimes,

35

You pushed my wheelchair more gently than anyone else,
no banging, no bumps. Cracked concrete of the old
Oakridge Mall, how we laughed and glanced at our hair,
our shining rosy fingernails in glass as we passed.

6.) *you say you're always "scrutinized" and yet I've never lectured,*
not Talk may be free. Penalties may be exacted afterward,
for years to come, in fact, depending on how uninhibited a
sib becomes.   But I have supported and comforted you,
agreed that plan after plan   Smell of your coffee, sun hot
as a body lying on me. Your newspaper on the white metal
table where you tossed it.

7.) *Doesn't that count? Please remember. When you'd come over*
Apologies can be received with glee.
now. I didn't at the time. Truly, I have loved you clearly as I
Green of junipers, far cottonwoods on the island to the
north of town. I perch uncomfortably on a concrete planter,
wait, look haughty while tears ease out behind sunglasses.
A hundred percent my fault? What can I say?
sad and say you felt better when you left?

LISTENING TO MY GRANDMOTHERS

I am waiting for my grandmothers
to tell me
if my sense of their lives is acceptable.
There are so many nuances:
white gloves, hats with half-veils,
how they talked to servants, tradespeople.
Rustle of their silky dresses.
The way they smelled sweetly
of face-powder.
I bend to catch
the flavour of their lives,
leisurely
with long afternoons.
I want to identify my grandmothers
in their incarnations
as schoolgirls
mothers
greying women who drew themselves up
for the camera, instantly recognizable
as They Who Must Be Appeased.
Bakers of apple pie
makers of mustard pickle
decent women who flew into loud rages
when terrified
or affronted.
Their cleanliness & evasions
carried over into my life as the possibility
of intense light
if only I can understand their secrets,
blue as bruises, as the unfurl of iris in sun.

I am leaning to my grandmothers.
I want to coax
their stories into tall stems that whisper.
Grandmothers, hear me,
I am
listening.

BURNING STONE

1

Donna, my Great-grandmother,
painted stags on china platters
watercolours of sailboats
& carved mahogany tables.
After five children,
she announced to her mainly-absent
Member-of-Parliament
husband
she wouldn't sleep with him again.
My mother raises her hand:
Daddy Frank, that was,
everyone knew what she'd said to him . . .
Donna didn't like children,
sent all hers once
to live with her sisters & brothers.
My mother's hand goes to her throat,
she smiles, memory bright,
as if those children found it hilarious too
and went off singing with clean socks
to houses that smelled
different
from their own
where they leaked tears on feather pillows
gulping like fish
to strain nourishment from hostile air.
Late at night, a hand or an arm
stuffed in mouths

so cousins wouldn't hear,
Mother Mother
don't you love me?
Daddy   Daddy
come back.

2

Rebellion, my mother says.
Donna always talked about not stopping
her pony when she was a child,
not doing what she was supposed to,
disobeying, she was a rebel
She liked me because I'd listen.

Great-Grandmother against the patriarchs!
My heart fires
predictably as a furnace
at a nudge on the thermostat.
All three daughters educated, RN's,
that was something in 1910.
Standing up to Daddy Frank
whose most memorable speech in political life
came when he rose in the House one afternoon
& said *Gentlemen, the Parliament buildings are on fire*
& people leapt to his words
obedient as leaves to a gust of hot wind.

3

Gramma, one of the five,
was the favourite
because she had curly hair.
In her sixties, she'd dip her head
the same way I have watched my mother
do, dip & preen
when she talked of Donna, queen of the cold
remark.
My hair is straight,
I'd never have been loved
in that jealous & flinty household.
Gramma mothered her two younger brothers.
One brother stole money from her.
She told me when I was eight,
would never mention his name again.
Didn't she remember
how children are pierced by memories
dark as skipping stones
recurring
again   again?

Gramma, who took me Christmas shopping
to Eaton's when I was six, seven & eight
who told me I was good company.
(I listened.)
Lunch was always the same
sliced hothouse tomatoes, the very best ground beef
orange Kraft dressing on both
with vanilla ice cream for dessert.
The structure of meals a ritual which
held back chaos
turned on the lights
made it look as though someone was home.
Gramma I loved you then.
I was proud of you.

4

Heroine of the First World War.
Nurse of the frontlines in France
where operating theatres were tents,
you told the story of the just-qualified doctor,
the green doctor you called him,
who insisted
on changing the dressing on the terribly injured soldier
who would let only you do it
because you were gentle.
The soldier begged the doctor,
moaned, finally screamed
    Nurse Glass
until the green doctor, male of course,
backed off, sweat streaming into his eyes
said *Finish it, nurse*
& triumphant, you came forward
to perform your miracle of sympathetic magic
& the green doctor
avoided you ever after.

Was that really how it went?
Or did the green doctor insist
on finishing those dressings
& then never bother you again?
I am sorry, I cannot
remember.
Certainly the injured soldier yelled
from a warm kitchen seat in your life-story
for the rest of your days.

5

Gramma, I never came to see you
those two years
you spent in Extended Care.
Most of the time you didn't open your eyes.
Mum said:
She wouldn't know you
& I grabbed her meaning like an undeserved present
& never did visit.
If it's any consolation, I am ashamed now.
You know what made me turn aside?
One day in the kitchen after you'd come
to live with us
you told the story of the green doctor again
& I realized
you hadn't nursed
for over forty years.
You didn't read
except for the Bible.
You'd given up going to church ten years before.
Even then, you had never helped out.
You didn't have one single friend.
How could I respect someone
who for forty years had given nothing
of herself to any cause or interest
greater than making meals?
I cut you out of my heart that morning,
pointed scorn
as if it were a shaman's bone
& I had power
to make candles leap & an old lady flutter
in the sulphur wind.

6

Before you moved in,
Mum had to call every night at seven
I saw you tethered—the umbilical cord
of the phone line in blue dusk
kept you from flailing off the globe.
If anything prevented Mum
I dreaded having to phone instead.
Mum would call at four to remind you
she'd have to be at a gallery opening, a meeting
but you'd still be angry, shouting
when I telephoned in the evening
You kids are no good to your mother,
No help to her at all.
You never do anything around the house
& your voice was so shaky & panic-
stricken, I'd stare at the wall phone
in the dark hall with the red *habitant* dresser
as if observing clearly enough
the holes, numbers,
the numbing black shape of the instrument
could fix the wrongness.
Where was the bond
of our best-ground-beef lunches?
Remember me, Gramma?
I do help, I do the ironing,
I'm good, really.
I'm only ten.

7

Later on, Mum called a family conference
about you moving in.
We were swollen with the lushness
of acting rightly.
Of course you should come
we were your FAMILY.
(Our own praise
curlicues of gold
& peacock feathers.)

Dad had gone to live on his own then.
In the morning,
after Mum left, my sister & brother & I
had undeclared war with you over the newspaper.
Who would reach the front porch first
after it was delivered?
If you won, all the sections
were lost to us:
in your room until we'd left for school
in the garbage when we got home
We had to go without sting of headlines,
eat breakfast without words
arid.
No, I haven't seen it I'd lie
when really I'd shoved my part of the paper
down behind the bench
the instant I heard your steps in the hall.
When I left I'd put it on the table
or knock on your bedroom door.
We got giddy, giggled, were sick
with ourselves, your fury
at the black game.
A few times
we tried sharing
but you didn't remember how.

After the stroke
Mum said you called her *Mummy*
said you seemed happy
to hold her hand & be mothered
by the nurses, your food came
& they spoon-fed you as you had your siblings.

8

My daughter is five now.
She had an aureole of soft curls when she was younger
hated it because grownups couldn't help
themselves, reached out to touch.
I thought of you, hoped her hair would straighten
so I could love her anyway.
The injustice of what Donna did to you
like scratches from blackberrying, still
smarting long after smears of juice
have been washed from arms.
Girl with the perfect ringlets
who had only natural curls to save you
from the wearisome crime of being a child,

I see my harshness.

I see farther than I used to, though
not with the elegant passion I would like
& I wish I could say
What happened?

Gramma, weren't you so angry you could spit steam?
Bored?
Your one wild girl
married off at sixteen,
that left you with only my mother

& the worst thing she ever did
was get kicked out of nursing school for pretending
to sleepwalk.
Didn't you boil
like tea water
when you got up in the morning,
demand something larger than the occasional apple pie
to conquer,
kitchen to be subdued
in an immaculate
blaze of surfaces?

9

It wasn't done in those days, my mother says.
Married women didn't work.
She tried to go back to nursing, we didn't
have much money
but they told her she'd have to take a course
a refresher.

I wish you had.
I wanted a burning stone
a woman wiser than the green doctor
a grandmother who blazed a way
I could pattern my life on.
I would have hung your days
on my wall
ancestral art
See those glowing colours,
eyes steady as a mountain?
She was a wonderful woman, my Gramma

lived to be eighty-eight
was active to the day she died
always giving of herself & much loved
by her community & grandchildren
especially me.
The picture was painted by her mother
Donna Glass, the famous turn-of-the-century
Ontario artist.

Donna had five children whom she adored
a successful career
a husband who was an MP.
He made such a memorable speech once
the Parliament buildings in Ottawa
were never the same afterward.
Inflammatory, you know.

BLACK FIRE

ONION ENRAGED

Wooo, that's strong
my mother might say, lighting a match
putting it, smoking,
between her lips
convinced
that when chopping an onion
an aureole of sulphur
rising to eye-level, makes her immune
to tears.

Onion enraged.
Raw onion
smelling up the kitchen
neat white bulb not shy
at claiming appreciation.

Come at me with a knife
I'm ready to roll anywhere
but diced for dancing
in your pan.

You may be sharp,
but I am a biting root
who wants a story
where the ending isn't already known
one of us crouched
on the maple cutting board
hissing   *sting sting.*

GENEALOGY OF COLOURS

When her husband says *No more,*
one child is enough
the woman's heart flies out the window
crying   White white
the edge of gulls' wings
against sky.
All the colours, she tells her daughter,
are in white.
The two of them imagine cracking white like an egg.
Out slide violet green blue
& their relations, refract from nearby trees.

I can't see any reason to.
His eyes are green & steady
the same as when she first brought him home
ten years ago
except
she can walk on that gaze now
& not fall through.

The wicker table has crumbs on it, broken strands.
Their coffee cups are empty,
absurd reminder of order when none exists
none at all
& her heart insists   White white.
She bats the noise away.
Damn it, they're still talking,
there's hope.

I'm too old,
he says.
She nods,

nods several times as he
makes his points.
She pulls her skin tighter for comfort
though it is too thin
& she is in darkness
out where the winter winds bluster
upside down on the clothesline
her own hesitations tangled
with red & yellow nursery rhymes,
the shout of White, white
lost mother-colour.
Liar
& deceiver
for not acknowledging her own
relief
that he has decided
for them, finally.
This is
expected pain
she has served the shadow of it
at her table, nightly.
At least her daughter is in bed
unable to say,
Why do you look like that, mommy?
The shadow has come home to roost, dear
& I would I had left it alone.

Tomorrow her child will ask,
Can we mix all the colours in the world
back together & get white?
When the woman goes to speak
lost colour will slip
from her silence
bright & falsely cheerful, flapping
in the brisk south-easterly wind.

PROPHET IN A HOSTILE LANDSCAPE

"...thine ears shall hear a word
behind thee, saying,
This is the way, walk ye in it."
                                        —*Isaiah*

this is the right air to swim in
you know by the flow
around your forehead
touch that says in a thousand
sensitive ways   *correct*
you a steelhead returning to the silver river
of utterance

this is the way to follow
you feel welcomed in its minute stops
between breaths

but the rocks come next
so suddenly
you forget how to differentiate

up from the rush of feeling
pectoral fins scraped down to the white bone
you whimper that you ever left
the salt smell & pull of bull kelp forests

for flesh of your flesh
you have given away safety
all the oxygen you treasured
you are not going upriver to spawn
not you, who have waited
while the Word you listened for
was silent

then came the numinous shift of air

& you followed

though ghost-daughters trail
faint as jellyfish filaments
you obey only the river,
& you have just water left
to say yes, yes
you have done
what is needful

& the fragrance of water
comforts, turbulent
you hold up your forehead, questing
your fins feel ruined
but that ache is secondary
you want assurance
to be given back the comfort of knowing
you move through the right
shape
of prophecy

ANCHORING THE SKY

The woman is firming a tree
in her heart, one of the cottonwoods
that flourish
down by the river,
bare branches black
against the sunset.
She & her husband drive
silently.
Her mind circles her shape
of tree.
For now, the woman has finished
crying:
the rest will depend on the tree.

Close to houses
cottonwoods are dangerous
their wood punky-looking orange.
The woman's seen enough
shattered stumps to know
these are not domestic trees;
last week, driving down this same
road, she saw one that had fallen
right across someone's kitchen
opened the roof to the resinous rush
of silver-backed leaves.
This week there is a *For Sale* sign up.
Though the tree has been bucked up
into firewood,
the house is no longer safe
for its owners:
who knows what further terrors
night holds in its windy hands?

The woman repeats
the tree's outline.
It is something hard
for her to circle,
helps to keep the night in place,
water in a bucket
spun round and round
to demonstrate gravity.
It might spray out
if spun too slowly.

The woman
& her husband seem to drive forever.
It finally becomes dark enough
she couldn't read if
she wanted to,
to the north,
the city's edges fold
around the pink-lit horizon.
She strokes cold branches for comfort.
The black prayer of her tree
anchors the sky.

DRAWING DOWN AIR

What matters
is getting down
intensity,
the woman rocking on a white bath mat
on the tub's edge
wishing she could throw up.

Even as she rubs one knuckle
across her mouth
the poem records the smell
of butter-fried sole, scrape of forks
against plates in the other room.
The demon-blue eye
she will stare at later
when she leaves the bathroom:
the TV which reigns
in the house across the street.
They have their own problems there.
Hey, retard, put your coat on,
someone calls to the blonde
seven-year-old she has seen dulling down
month after month.

What matters right now
is how
the woman escapes
from the poem.
She is cold on her unlit stairwell.

The noise of forks stops.
At length the woman gets up
stiffly
gropes her way into the bedroom
finds a pen.
Now she can draw down air
cut her own shapes
against the dark.

SONG OF THE RIVER

The woman fears
the river.
She feels it summoning her
at night.
Pure cold syllables.
The woman is too hot.
She thinks of slipping on cold
a dark moving mouth
filling her own.
The song of river becoming her own.

The woman fears
choking,
leaving her warm bed,
waking her husband still asleep beside her,
someone seeing her
in her dressingown
as she slips across the road
to the river,
streetlights humming,
angular stems of rosebushes
unforgiving
against the red-painted net shed
on the bank.

The woman fears
grey
in survivors' hearts,
the soft *quonk quonk* of ducks
disturbed along the bank.
Her daughter feeds those ducks.
If she listens to the river
who would be there to console
that child?
To open arms
gather her in,
whisper endless mother-comfort
in all its soft colours:
There, there, it will be all right.

SMELL OF HOT METAL

The woman's marriage throbs
like a blood blister.
Seeing it, she feels
flutters of breathlessness;
the opossum she'd seen
the morning before, huddled
on the median in rush-hour traffic.
Its pink tail scaley,
body frozen, not knowing
the meaning of *maladaptive*
                neocortex
           not working.

The woman's marriage is saturated
with panic
familiar as waking
at 3 am.
It is a poor idea
to put on pain
as if it were velour,
warm from the dryer.

The blister, black beneath the nail.
Nowhere for the swelling to go.

Time for a needle & pliers
she thinks
not knowing if the match she holds
will cauterize the silver metal,
if she is up to forcing the needle
through.

POPLAR

Perhaps because she is tired
the poplar outside the window
startles her so.
All night long she has fled
from one dream
to another,
heart firing unevenly as a junky car,
red nightie sweat-wet.
Now she has clothed herself
in day's calm
until the poplar five feet away
lunges
& she jerks back in her chair,
ashamed:
between them, glass,
safety of the expected;
the room full of books,
her blue knapsack on the table beside her.

All that reaches
are fingers, dormant
at this time of year.
Shaking, she turns
from their dark bark.

TREES

Wherever she goes,
trees talk to her
in anguished swaying,
their stark language of form

visible
against pale walls,
black arms empty
in the season
before renewal.

The south-easterly whips
fiercely
against the woman's unprotected legs.
Half-running, she fears
for her umbrella
flinches as though trees have
trained her to her own size:

Duck
Make yourself small
We'll hit you

though they haven't yet.
They are only
leafless shapes,
bare dreams following her
into day.

BLACK FIRE

I am in the black fire,
the dread my family
edges around,
the abyss, the roaring black.
No one told me it made so much noise.

I cannot think
for the sound of it.
I endure, I try
to pray.
My books lie to one side
of the striped couch.
Blackness, clamouring.
The heat.

This is the shape
we will not trace with words
though we think it
every time one of us despairs.
If we mention it
we might conjure terror.
Once more the fire, smouldering,
will leap & call.
Each relative gone
marks more clearly
the devouring path.

I cannot sleep.
Around me, black fire flares.

INSTRUCTIONS TO MY FAMILY

When the black fire finds you
think of it as a personal demon
which claims
to belong to us.

Other families have their own guises
of dread.

This one
is never spoken of in case
it gulps someone
on their way home from the library,
anticipating the lights of home.

It's the part of us that falls in love,
wakes up wanting
to go for a swim one sunny morning in July,
gone wrong.
The dream-side of the brain
deteriorated, gaunt & reeking.

Think a thing you'll meet one evening,
dry horror
when radiation makes the forest floor
sick. Engulfing salal grows
blighted, pallid.
Think a place where your own thought turns sick.

It will happen suddenly
a black wave breaking
over your head.

Think of it, not as inhabiting fire,
but a mask.
Pass through.

INSTRUCTIONS FROM THE DEAD

1

It is important to remember the dark fire
ringing your horizon
has nothing to do with you.
Sure, it claims
your life is a long October night
when frost crouches low to earth
& all the annuals wake up black
& spongy with ruptured cells.

You are not a marigold.

2

Others have passed through.
Some of us
failed, but by no means
all.
Hang onto small magics
the green cleanliness of basil.
Rub the smell on your fingers,
then remember
the way a child runs to hug
you after an absence,
a windmill, arms flailing,
face alight.

3

The leaves are for the healing
of nations.
That's you, too.
All the burned bits
cooled with leaves
surprising everyone
by turning into
elastic vine, stronger than steel
than spider web, fit
for anything you want to build.

4

Yes, we died
from this fire.
Some of us ran into it
& burned,
some of us ran away,
with clothes a-light & minds
quite gone,
knowing only pain
& the need to escape.

5

That said, the key is to disbelieve
in the fire—
illusion dropped heavily
on one generation
by another.
An invisible legacy.
We are sorry.
Despise the ring walls,
pass through.
You are much larger than you believe
& more powerful.
Silver is the colour of coolness.
Press it against your heart
go valiantly,
for those who love you
are greater in number
& dearer than darkness.

6

From the sidelines, all of us cheer you.
In the kitchen, your family smiles
at you over the remains of dinner;
they can't see the flames
know only that something troubles
the evening's peace,
& they extend care,
quickly, as you would shoot out an arm
if you saw your mother
stumble.

7

This is the worst.
There is no more.
To stare at those towering
walls of black breaking above
& say *that which I greatly feared has come upon me*.
Onward.
There is still delight in the world
though you cannot perceive it,
still the green & geranium reds
of gardens,
though for you, all the colours
are seen through the bleak filter of fire.
Go through.
We are cheering you
& safety is nearer—almost underfoot—
than you in your struggles
believe possible.

A NEW SONG

THE DAY IS YOUR HOME

The day is a tent
green as glacier melt
into which you pull the world.
Grass, tall as a child against sky.
Foxgloves, significant
in pink, the ground wears
like wands.
The man who thrashes in bed
at night
warm & hurried, his body
arches toward day.
Walls erect themselves
in waves of sweet-smelling lumber
while he sleeps
& strains.

The day is your home
tilting.
You wake into it,
sap slow with morning cold
but running,
& you, you must allow
recognition to push
through your skin
green & overhead.

PURITY 1

Purity has white feet.
Purity lives in May,
fragrance of mock-orange bushes
silky red of Oriental poppies
against a cedar fence.
Early morning.

Purity doesn't ask anyone's permission
to be joyous.
Purity turns the world,
silvery stem
in the blue-green apple of Earth.

Purity gets it right
the first time.
White feet
twirl
at eye's edge.

PURITY 2

Purity comes in white handfuls,
smells like clothes gathered in dry
from the line.
Purity is puffed
weighs nothing.
Purity appears when you are least
expecting it.
Opened, it foams
around broken skin
the corner of your mind which mourns
anything,
the old Russian Blue cat, blind
in one eye,
the amount of money you owe
in back taxes.
Purity is impersonal.
It arrives from the Milky Way
daily.
Purity wants to come & live
with you
fill whole rooms
with spongy white,
mop up night.

PORTENT

Waiting for inspiration
sweet as the fragrance
of *Nelly Moser* clematis,
starfish flowers
pink stripes upturned to
slow slide-by of air
as the globe rotates
in its silver scarf of atmosphere.

Waiting.
A hummingbird.
Silence of its leaving.
Waiting
as if the glossy *mahonia* leaves
held a secret.
For certainty
to rise, rich
as light, a bubble
to bounce inside.

For the faint comfort of a distant lawnmower
to reveal the Word.
A shovel turning over dry earth
to show incalculable meaning,
the world,
a significant worm.

SHUTTING THE DOOR

The room you tell me to go into is resonant with antique
Afghan wall-hangings, brown, magenta & cream   You
say the room is big as my imagining; it is my fancy to have
the walls white, the sun through the east window soft &
July

The room is a forest   Holly, wild cherry & the hot
drowsy resin of pine, crinkle of old needles
underfoot   Feathery run of an ant across one cheek

I do not dream the room, I receive it from the elegant
complexity of intelligence that creates spiral
galaxies   Shimmer of massed suns

There is no malice of matter   At night, the wall-hangings
do not rise up & writhe from star to star for the sheer
pleasure of seeing me defeated: where have all their colours
gone?

Wool, inert, the weavings clasp their wooden dowels meek
as Christmas holly berries, true red echoing in my heart
long after the prick of leaves against pale winter sky has
passed, sluff of footsteps on the drum of ground

THE VISION CENTRE

to enter again seeing
a place with many drawers
rooms full of visions you pull out
deep as charts

memo: your vision
has arrived, perfect & glowing

shared visions, a house in the country
complete with *Etoile Violette* clematis
the peace of abundant greenery

redoing the vision
polishing up
smartening to acceptable vision standards

revising vision
say again, see again, hear again vision

born again vision

vision with lemon oil

vision clothed with clematis
eyes open, repeating ragged purple stars

HOREB REVISITED: *OR* FIVE WAYS TO WALK RIGHT BY A BURNING OBJECT*

for Geoffrey

1

Ignore it.
Spontaneous combustion never happens
to someone
you know.

2

Transfix it with
contempt.
What, you, to be caught
believing
in leaping warmth
of holiness?

3

Call it art.

4

Call it light,
a trick of irritated photons,
by definition an illusion.

5

Tamp the probability index
down to zero.
Gaze straight at flame
make your eyes
recant
orange.

*[See Exodus 3, 4:17]

PEELING BACK THE WORLD

I reach down to the turning world   The layer which
today, slips aside so easily, continents, oceans, albacore in
their schools of dark-eyed silver

Mother of lights with whom there are no variables   It is
I who live in shadows & despair

Go through, go through the gates   Behind sunsets, the
peach clouds puffy against the valley walls   Peel back
geology, the layers of an onion   Deeper

White against green, I tumble or am carried   Adoration
of a dead Siamese cat a focus momentarily, a prism of fawn
fur with me; this is the sea beyond stars he drew
from   The infinity cradle

Ah, substance, this is where the tender world stops turning

WATER FOR A TONGUE

for Marjorie

What can I give you, sister, but what I so often fail at:
words, the ropes between what I really mean
& the thing itself, hanging like a bridge
over a mountain stream
one end of which has been
torn away.

We laugh at ourselves, you & I.
Brave sounds, we use them around the awkwardness
of never knowing what is expected of us
by ourselves least of all.

When my husband tells me
he's put the jack
through the rocker panel of my car,
15 years of love for that vehicle rust-rotted
through,
it is your fierce cherishing
of aged vehicles
I think about
when I laugh.

You, of all people,
will appreciate what light
I threw into air then.
Laughter makes a good noise in the night,
better than choking
on the smell of onions or apples
or the bald slipperiness
of us with no money to stop
disintegration.

When I fumble with words for you
trying to comfort or cheer,
I wish I had water for a tongue,
maybe then we'd understand one another
more clearly.
Perhaps this is all you & I can do,
love one another from opposite sides
of rushing tenderness.

HERON'S NEST

for Richard Beaufort Simmins

1   Spinning

I am anxious you like this poem.
It's meant to be served with a *whissht*
of cappuccino for grownups,
for the children
hot chocolate & whipped cream, the kind you used to buy
me at Woolworths when I grew old enough to walk.
Glorious fascination of red stools
how they spun
exactly as I twirl an apple
from its stem
over the sink.

Here is an apple
satisfying as the whole-hearted hug
of a child.

On our last visit
you couldn't eat Greek salad
rough with green peppers & cucumbers.
I don't want you to go
where letters aren't delivered.
Stay where I know how to find you.
I want to find words
to describe this untidy heron's nest
of tenderness I carry toward you, my father,
who always believed
I could spin straw to gold.

2   Prophet

Twenty-one years dry, you have tried so hard
to make restitution
for the abandonment
your first set of children are still
forgiving you for.
You who warn us
what to expect
what treachery & bloody-mindedness wait,
how we are descended from visionaries & gamblers.
Listen, you say
raising an index finger:
Let me tell you
about the way things work.

I don't laugh anymore.
Your predictions are almost always right,
though your lack of hope
I lay aside
overwhelming as skin raw across mouth
& eyes.
Seer.
Your sadness makes my innards burn.
(Soft agitation of a slug
I put salt on once.)
As long as I can remember,
you have been playing the wise ancient
& now you are
white-haired, lean on the outside
of the dark doorframe we all must pass
through.
You peek in, tell us
the universe's secrets.

3   Paring Down to Song

At fleamarkets you still look for books,
buy black & white hand-carved
cows.
I think of you surrounded
by the clean singing of a well-run house;
rich blues of Indian tablecloths.
Prints & paintings by young artist friends
crowd hallways.
You live in the order
of whimsical wooden airplanes
& your new wife welcomes all
your children.

Against the dark you burn candles.
(The oldest male in the family
for three generations, you say,
lighting a fresh cigarette.)
You worry you haven't accumulated
more, a house, new furniture, vast handwoven carpets
like your wealthy artist colleague, but you have showed me
not to be afraid to start again.
All a person needs, you say, *is a few pieces of art*
a couple of beautiful rugs & some good pottery.
More than once
I have watched you give the rest away
& you have not withered
you send out new shoots.
I am a very spiritual man,
you have told me.
I believe you, the hurting come
to your store for miles around, for comfort.
I am a sitting duck for men with problems,
you observe in one letter, *but I'm getting too old . . .*

4   Gravenstein

This is the poem I should have written you
the first time. A Gravenstein fresh
from the tree, my teeth sink into an apple
satisfying as the wholehearted hug
of a child.
I was going to say
your teeth sink into crispness
but I remembered how few you have left.
I don't want to hurt your feelings!
I want you to say *Feel this poem*
my daughter made
Isn't it round & pleasing to the hands
perfect as an apple in autumn?

You try so hard to live
a good moral life
while grumbling you are NOT a sweet man.

Our frothy cappuccinos are done.
I think of you, of apples
streaky & heaped into hills at Rideau Market,
smile, crinkle-eyed at
the you of my imagination, forever expounding.
I pretend we are exchanging smiles.
I hold onto mine for a long time,
savour the rounded moment.

PERSONAL: WOMAN SEEKS SAFETY FOR PERMANENT COMPANIONSHIP

Safety would be cool, with silver fur.
Safety would take her dancing
to a place where marsh marigolds
bloomed.
It would be sunny
& morning, the ground would squelch
joyously underfoot.
Safety would smooth her hair.
Safety would love her
without passion
as if she were a white tiger-lily
or water
shining through distant trees.

GIFTS MY MOTHERS, MY GRANDMOTHERS
GIVE ME

for Barbara Jeannette Simmins

1

Love of the deep cleanliness of older women   Integrity
reassuring as the smell of ironing, warm as the just-pressed
shirt my mother commands me to go find a hanger
for   Steady way mothers work, not guerilla warfare with
the vacuum cleaner, hit & run, but actual moving of
furniture to get behind   Hot baths & rose talcum powder

2

Secret of arrival   I adopt grandmothers, one for
knowledge of Latin plant names, the way we cosily talk
flowers for hours, another seen a moment in the produce
store, fleecy turquoises & greens & white hair, joy in her
face   There is some stillness in these unsurprised eyes I
hunger for, so different from my own gritty dissatisfactions

3

Capability with rhythm of a shovel, skipping a
generation   Delight of April sun on shoulder blades,
planning vehemence of scarlet climbing roses & giant silver
lilies, mignonette for back-of-the-border fragrance   My
maternal grandfather used to take visitors to see his wife's
shelves of gleaming jars in the basement, all the rich colours
of harvest   *There weren't stores then the way there are now,* my
mother says *What mother put up was what we ate, all winter long*

4

Endless frugality   Surprise of finding my own staples,
potato soup, lentil soup, in my paternal grandmother's 1926
diary under Winter Meals   *Never waste food   Think of
the starving children in India,* she'd say when I couldn't eat my
fishsticks Like most kids, I was all for exporting
leftovers   Thirty-odd years later, & her sawing at
consciousness has sunk so deep I save even heels of bread
to grind into crumbs, make bread-puddings   Queen of
left-overs

5

The gift of terror   Omnipotent old women, children &
clerks scurried when my grandmothers drew themselves up
on their dignity   Like King Canute who tried to
command the waves, they could be encroached on only so
far   They succeeded, believe me   Some vital secret of
assertion must have been lost, though, or I misunderstood
the snap of grey heads, flaring of outraged nostrils   My
grandmothers made dominion look so easy   The struggle
I have had to tame my terrible mouth, trying to succeed to
their authority

6

Spiritual leadership   Augusta, in her eighties, who
visited the long-term care hospital every Saturday, played
the piano, did the patients' hair, fed people younger than
she was   Aunt Rose, ninety-one, who has finally given
up mowing her own grass but forks up gifts from her
garden, red tulip bulbs, autumn crocus & lily of the valley
Now if they don't grow, you come back & I'll dig you up some more,
you hear? Mary Louise, whose age I wouldn't dare ask, goes
to every environmental hearing for miles around, writes
letters to save estuaries, reuses liners from her cereal box
Much better than the wax paper you can buy   She tells me
crisply when I mumble

7

Women of power, & mine   Mine because we are kin in
giving, ancient as ox-eye daisies, as pervasive   Innocent
in ditches, white along storm-swept islands on the outer
coast where surf never stops booming   Not delphiniums,
unreliable aristocrats of the garden, nor weeds, my mothers
are hardy perennials, beautiful & utilitarian women whose
hands flower continually with issues, with food &
lace   Truly my mothers are powerful beings   I hope
one day, to thicken up into growth worthy of them, poke
sprigs of scarlet *crocosmia* into soft water-scented air

A NEW SONG

1

To forgive . . . that I may be forgiven,
my father writes.
A burst of bells. What are we?
Sum of our lives, years & years of giving or not
or a few key gut-wrenching moments of anger
shame, melodrama?
We make reparations for those moments
for years.
They ring through the rest of our lives.

My own towering furies, red rage of a berserker
blood vessels in my eyes engorged
until all I saw was red
& I leapt upon the sister who taunted me . . .
Ah, justifications.
She's dead. I didn't kill her.
I worried I might, by accident in one of our fights.
She killed herself two weeks after her twentieth birthday
barbiturates large enough, finally,
in a submarine world.

The young cop at the door
coarse-textured navy pants
a moustache. His moustache was earnest
trying to find out her birthday, not approximate but exact
me trotting back & forth between the kitchen
with its shabby linoleum & tiled counters
where we were talking
& the living room, where Aunt Anne was comforting
Mum.

I offered everyone tea & aspirin.

2

Self-acceptance amidst chaos,
my father says in a letter.
Humour, great music, books, ideas . . . co-existing
with poverty & desperation.
He is trying to rescue my grandfather.
Last week I dug him up & excoriated him in a poem,
spat on his bones for what he did to my uncle.
Now my father is whisking dirt from the skeleton
He writes flesh
on the bones,
dresses my grandfather as he was in life,
natty grey flannels, tweed jacket, tie, hat.
. . . a fine-looking man, always the Major.

3

My grandfather, co-author of the Kemmis-Simmins report
of 1928. In it he recommended the abolition
of patronage appointments to the Canadian Civil Service.
Merit as the basis of hiring.
For this, he was fired,
& with three children & a wife to support, blackballed.
He never worked again.

This is the man I wouldn't forgive.

This man was whipped by his mother
with a riding crop,
left home when he was fourteen
with a scholarship
to Glen Almond University, Scotland.
He never forgave his mother, the original Zoë.
She married again, quickly, after her doctor husband died,
left her forty Australian pounds in debt.
Zoë had no means of support,
three children
& a great black stallion for whom the crop
was originally intended.
Nicodemus she called him, a devil's name.
My grandfather was named after the horse.
Nick hated his step-father,
a canon in the Church of England.
After he emigrated,
Nick kept the circle of unforgiveness
spinning & sharp,
wrote neither his mother
nor his twin brothers.

4

Mandrax, that's what my sister died
from. It took me ten years
to hear her laughter going out the livingroom window,
how the house rung
& swung for joy!
I had to forgive her
myself
thirty or forty times.
I thought it would never end.
That morning the weight of Karen
slipped from me:
I heard her,
& the fine imprint of skin,
the feel of her was fresh in air,
the way you feel someone
who's just gone out of the room.

5

The last time we fought,
Karen nearly won.
It scared me.
She'd been off everything but methadone
for a couple of years,
& had grown strong
mucking out her horse's stall.
Then I realized she expected me to win:
I was in the right.
Always.
If I hadn't hated her so much,
my heart would have thumped me,
a swollen fist leaking pity
& thin pink tears.

After each fight,
I'd swear never again.
Ashes & vinegar,
the hot strong taste of anger
ebbing
to self-disgust.
No more ending up on floors,
having to stop myself from thunking Karen's head
on their cold hardness:
Don't do it again!

At the end of each fight,
I was left with the certainty of my awfulness,
my sister's depravity.
I had to pack these up heavy
& stinking as suitcases full of rotten herring,
carry them around
& be cheerful.
Or attempt it.

6

To recall only this
is totally to distort one's history, my father writes.
Hence the importance
of my grandfather's careful dressing;
what had he really to get dressed for?
Nick was an educated man, a classical scholar.
Fired for honesty,
at less than forty years of age
his working life was over.
He was a binge drinker,
excelled at gardening.
He never complained, my father says,
never
& he never swore.

We bumble along in these bodies,
are faced with consequences
of what they've done
at every turn.
We.
Actions we'd like to disown.
As I grow into wisdom (surely I will?)
I'd like to be able to discern
each challenge
limpid as green water seen from ten feet up on
a dock.
& act with integrity.
No cringing afterward.
The daily battles
are our practices.
Small courages repeated
like Nick not complaining.
Like forgiveness.

There has to be a solid *chunk* of a door
shutting
a new one opening.
Nick might have called me a guttersnipe
for fighting.
Last week I railed at him for being a child molester,
unforgivable.
There are always accusations
to throw.
I don't want to anymore.
I want the whole cycle of family blame
inflamed self-righteousness
to come to a stop
punctured.
Wheels spinning, to slow, slow,
silver knives not turning anymore.

I've also learned to forgive . . .
in the hope that one or two generations hence
I too may be forgiven, my father writes.
My sister's laughter,
& it was friendly, happy
as I seldom remember her being,
went out the window.
I felt blessed,
light as a balloon.
Nick, you too, I will let go.

At the finish of a love letter to my grandmother
you used to write in Greek
ἀεὶ, ἀεὶ, εἰς τοὺς αἰωνὰς τῶν αἰωνῶν
Always, always, into the twilight of the ages.
I see you out for a stroll in this long twilight,
jaunty of shoulder,
bleak of eye,
as cheerful as you can be under the circumstances.
The Major.
With walking stick.
No one enjoys having one's dignity of life jostled
& totally forgotten
by a revisionist grandchild.
All the great Bach symphonies
silent.

7

The bones I was so careless with,
I will rebury.
You are not them,
but courtesy never goes amiss.
I am willing to begin
forgiving.
How long it takes I won't know until
it's over.

I guess we have forever.

THE DEAD RISE IN US

The dead rise in us
fragrant as pine
& green with needles of stories
they never did fathom.

Our work is to chart
the reefs, the sweet
deep-water passages.
What's the plot line?

The dead wait, anxious as children at bed-time,
to see how their stories will finish this time.
The shame they told only one person about.
The great plucked strengths beneath the hurt.

Our ancestors don't tell us, though, that our narratives
grow rooted from theirs, or can't,
in that thin eyeblink universe away
from flesh.

Time means nothing to the dead.
Getting it right does,
emotions which still batter the living,
gnarled lies, the distress we mistake for our own.

 The sheer bright energy
 the dead wasted thinking themselves
 animals in cold houses
 they laboured endlessly to warm.

 Suffering. Lost.

So they give the luminous tail-ends
to us. Red columbines flowering
at fifteen hundred feet, above a mountain lake,
rasp of breath as we pull ourselves higher.

Not that the dead focus upon us,
they are somewhere between air
sweet from that lake
& the pinwheel of fresh-minted galaxies,
Resolving whatever problems the fleshless encounter.
Hoping that this time, the stories come out
undistorted.
Theirs. Ours. Wood with no knots.

Solving the stories. Absolving. Clear water beneath.
Pine in the sunshine, the gusts we have of *knowing*
when we let the dead speak.
Our grandfathers died despising their failings—

An insight which lifts us practically off the path
as we bite down hard on feelings we had thought ours.
Clues.
There is a right shape to be here,

One not made with hands.
As if our kindnesses reach backward
& touch them. As one day descendants
may comfort us.

Lupines, still blooming at high elevations
their glorious blue
the colour of forgiveness,
of stories that grow clear.

About The Author

Zoë Landale lives in Ladner, B.C. with her husband and young daughter. Landale's work has appeared in many magazines, both literary and mass market. Her poems, fiction and non-fiction have been published in over twenty anthologies and have won a number of awards, among them a National Magazine Gold for a memoir, and first prize in short fiction from the University of Stony Brook, New York. Landale is a founding member of the Work Writers' Union, and a former President of the Federation of B.C. Writers. She has an MFA in Creative Writing from the University of British Columbia.